Kids On Earth

A Children's Documentary Series Exploring Human Culture & The Natural World

Chile

Sensei Paul David

COPYRIGHT PAGE

Kids On Earth - A Children's Documentary Series Exploring Global Cultures & The Natural World: Chile
by Sensei Paul David,

Copyright © 2023

All rights reserved.

978-1-77848-381-3 KoE_Chile_Ingram_HardbackBook

978-1-77848-380-6 KoE_Chile_Ingram_PaperbackBook

978-1-77848-379-0 KoE_Chile_Amazon_PaperbackBook

978-1-77848-378-3 KoE_Chile_Amazon_eBook

This book is not authorized for free distribution copying.

www.senseipublishing.com

@senseipublishing
#senseipublishing

Get Our FREE Books Now!

kidsonearth.life

kidsonearth.world

Click Below for Another Book In Each Series

senseipublishing.com/KoE_SERIES

senseipublishing.com/KoE_Wildlife_SERIES

KoE En Español

senseipublishing.com/KoE_SERIES_SPANISH

www.senseipublishing.com

Join Our Publishing Journey!

If you would like to receive FUTURE FREE BOOKS and get to know us better, please click www.senseipublishing.com and join our newsletter by entering your email address in the pop-up box.

Follow/Like/Subscribe: Facebook, Instagram: @kidsonearth

Scan the QR Code with your phone or tablet to follow us on social media:

Like / Subscribe / Follow

Welcome to Chile!

My name is Sofia and this is my brother Matias.

Matias and I would love to take you on a trip through our beautiful country, Chile. It is a very special place, and we cannot wait to share it with you.

Are you excited? Let's Go!

FUN FACTS

The official name of Chile is the Republic of Chile and the residents of Chile call themselves Chileans.

Chile has a small population, only around 18 million. Most of Chile resides in the capital city Santiago. The population has a large number of children, around 28% in total.

Some of the other places that you will find most of the residents of Chile are:
- Greater Santiago
- Greater Concepcion and
- Greater Valparaiso

Most of the residents in Chile live close to the middle of the country, meaning that we are a centralized country.

Let us look at your country.
Where do the people mainly live?
Are they mainly along the coastline or do they live in the Mountains or the middle like Chile?

FUN FACTS

The capital city Santiago is named after the biblical character St. James. It was named Santiago in 1541 by conquistador Pedro de Valdivia.

The Chilean people are a mix of Spanish and Native Americans. Today only 30% of the population refer to themselves as being mestizo or of mixed ancestry. Only 11% refer to belonging to an indigenous group.

> Matias, that is an unusual word, ancestors. What does that mean?

> Excellent question Sofia!
> Ancestor means the people that came before us. This means people like our parents, our grandparents, and our great grandparents.
> We are their descendants.

Do you know where your ancestors come from?
Maybe check with your mum, dad, or grandparents
And discover where your ancestors come from.

FUN FACTS

After Chile received independence in 1818 the Mapuche Communities were cast-out, becoming second-class citizens in their own country. Some of the other indigenous groups in Chile are called the Rapa Nui who live on Easter Island and the Aymara People.

Chile is a long country. It is one of the longest countries in the world. It measures a whopping 4.329 kilometers or 2689.916 miles long from north to south.

Chile just misses out on being the longest country in the world. Russia is longer east to west, and Brazil is slightly longer north to south.
But Chile can claim the title of the narrowest country. It is only 180 kilometers or 111.85 miles from east to west.

Time to look at a map!
Can you find out how long Russia is and
How long Brazil is?

With a grown-up's help, you are going to need
2 maps. After you have these maps, find Chile and carefully cut
Around the country. Now can you place Chile inside Russia or Brazil?

FUN FACTS

Chile is the seventh longest of the twelve countries in South America.

Chile is known as a hotspot for earthquakes to where it is located. Chile is located within the Ring of Fire and the Nazca Plate between the South American Plate.

Since 1501 there have been 46 known earthquakes with an estimated magnitude of 8.5 or higher around the world, and one-third of these took place in Chile.

What is your country known for? Do you have Earthquakes, tsunamis, floods, fires, or Any other natural disasters?

**Time to do some research!
What do you know about the origins of earthquakes?
Have you heard about Tectonic Plates?**

FUN FACTS
Indonesia holds the record for the highest number of earthquakes. Chile holds the record for the largest Earthquake ever record.

In 1960 the Valdivia Earthquake shook Chile at a magnitude of 9.4-9.6.

In 1888 Easter Island become a part of Chile. But Easter Island is nowhere near Chile! It is located in Polynesia. That is 3 510 kilometers or 2 180 miles away.

Easter Island is one of the world's most remote islands in the world. It takes 5.5 hours to fly from Santiago to Mataveri International Airport.

Easter Island is well known for its Giant Stone Statues.
Easter Island is also called Isla de Pascua or Rapa Nui.

Time to do some research!
Can you find the Giant Stone Statues that Easter Island is
Well known for on the internet?
Do not forget to ask your parents for help and for permission to use the Internet.

FUN FACTS

Easter Island is one of the world's most remote islands. It takes 5.5 hours to fly from Chiles' capital city of Santiago to Mataveri International Airport on Easter Island

Chile often has its flag confused with the Texan Flag of America.

Both flags have a white and red stripe with a white star. But the Chilean flag has a blue square in the top left corner, and the Texan flag has a blue stripe down the left side of the flag.

What does the flag of your country look like?
What colors are in your flag?
Does your flag share any similarities with any other country?

FUN FACTS

The Chilean Flag is 22 years older than the Texan flag. The Chilean Flag also has an Emoji, whereas the Texan flag has not had one made!

The official language of Chile is Spanish.

We would like to share some phrases and words with you so you can say hello as well!

- **Hola** – Hello or **Buenas** – Hi (informal)
- **Buenos días** – Good morning
- **Buen día** – Good morning (less common, used in Argentina)
- **Buenas tardes** – Good afternoon
- **Buenas noches** – Good evening
- **Bienvenido** – Welcome

Is there something special about the way you write in your language? Do you use special symbols or characters?

FUN FACTS

In Spanish, we invert or turn the question and exclamation marks upside down when we write! We have given you some examples for you to look at:
1. **¡Buenos días!** – Good morning!
2. **¡Bienvenido!** – Welcome!
3. **¡Que gusto de verlo!** – What a pleasure to see you!

15

The Chilean government is a Republic. A Republic government is one where the country is ruled by a representative of the citizens. This means, that modern republic governments believe that their people are the sovereigns. But they have representatives speak for them in government matters.

Chile celebrates its independence on the 18th of September.
Does your country have a day of independence?
What does this day mean to you and your country?

FUN FACTS

Chile's national anthem is Himno Nacional de Chile which translates to Anthem of Chile.
We also have National Day, the 18th of September.

GOVERNMENT CHILE

Mattias and I would like to share some of our National Symbols.

We have three national colors
1. Red
2. White
3. Blue

Our national flower is the Copihue, our national bird is the Condor, and our national animal is called the Huemul.

Another name for the Huemul is the South Andean Deer. The South Andean Deer is one of the two mid-sized deer and lives in the high mountains and the cold valleys of the Andes.

Can you tell Sofia and me what your national symbols are?
With a grown-up's help, find a photo of the following animals:
- **Pudu**
- **Kodkod**
- **Condor and**
- **South Andean Deer.**

Can you draw one of these animals?

FUN FACTS

Chile is home to the largest bird prey, the condor, and to the smallest deer called the Pudu and the smallest cat, the Kodkod, within South America.

Most of Chile identifies as Christian, some of the other religions that you will find in Chile are:
- Catholic
- Protestant and
- Jehovah's Witness

The indigenous citizens, the Mapuche, continue to follow the religion of their ancestors. These tales of their beliefs have been passed down orally for generations. Depending on the region and territory of the Mapuche clan, some variations can be found within their beliefs.

What does your religion believe?
Do you believe in heaven and hell?

FUN FACTS

In the Mapuche beliefs there are three vertical or spiritual planes. These are called:
1. Wenu Mapu refers to the land above. This can be referred to in some beliefs as heaven.
2. Nag Mapu which is the earthly plane. This is where humans and nature inhabit.
3. Minche Mapu to the underworld or in some place this is known as Hell.

Chile is home to a large range of natural terrains. This includes ancient glaciers, snow-white salt plains, and the driest desert on Earth. You can also find forests, lakes, and active volcanoes.
The driest desert is called the Atacama Desert, and only receives 12 millimeters or 0.47 inches of rain per year.
This makes the Atacama Desert the driest non-polar desert, and the second-driest desert in the world. It is the only desert to receive less rain than the polar deserts.

> Sofia. Can you tell our readers what a polar desert is?

> Sure Mattias. Polar Deserts are deserts at the Earths Poles or where it is cold. This means that the Antarctic and the Arctic are both deserts.

> That is very interesting. I did not know that the Arctic and Antarctic were deserts. Did you reader? Sofia, then what is a non-polar desert is?

> A non-polar desert is one made of sand instead of ice. Places like the Sahara Desert, the Arabian Desert, and the Atacama Desert here in Chile.

There are 23 deserts in the world.
With an adults' help, can you find the names of all the deserts?
After you have found them all, place them in order of Smallest to biggest.

FUN FACTS

NASA uses the Atacama Desert and a special place called the Valle de la Luna or the Moon Valley to test its instruments for future Mars Missions.

"Mattias, was that your stomach I heard grumbling? With all this learning, I can see why you are so hungry. While you fix us a snack Mattias, I can tell the reader about some of the delicious foods here in Chile."

Due to the wide variety of ecosystems in Chile, we have a wide variety of different food that we can eat.

Our favorite dish is the national dish, which is called Cazuela de ave. Cazuela is a soup that is made with meat, and root vegetables. It is made with peppers, chili, and corn. It is a great dish for winter.

Mattias, can you tell our readers what an Ecosystem is?

An ecosystem is where different things connect together in a physical environment. Things like animals and plants and the land they live in.

Did you know that Avocado was a fruit?
What makes an Avocado a piece of fruit?

FUN FACTS

Chileans love Avocados! We love this fruit that we try to make sure we eat it in all our meals. For breakfast, we have this on French bread, with a little bit of oil and salt. We also put it in salads, pizza, pasta, and sushi.

Chileans have four meals a day. The largest is usually eaten during lunch time.
We have a special name for our later meal. It is called *once*. We eat this meal between 5pm and 9pm which can also be called tea time.
Some of the more common foods we eat during this time are:
- Bread
- Jam
- Meat
- Cheese
- Avocado
- Pate
- Cake

And we drink coffee or tea.

Do you have any rules when it comes to mealtime?
How many meals a day do you eat?

FUN FACTS

there are some basic rules in Chile that we all observe.
Some of our eating rules are:
- If you eat at someone else's place, you wait for the host to show you to your seat,
- You are not allowed to eat until the host invites you
- Both hands need to be visible during the mealtime
- If you take more than you can eat it is classified as impolite and
- It is impolite to refuse a drink.

Do you like swimming? Chile is home to the second-largest swimming pool in the world. The swimming pool can be found at San Alfonso del Mar, a private resort in Algarrobo, Chile. It is about 100kilometerss or 62 miles west of Santiago.

The pool was built in 2006, is 1013 meters or 3 323 ffeetlong, and is 8.2 hectares or 20 acres in total. It holds 250 million litres, or 66 million US gallons of salt water, and is 35 meters deep, or 114.8 foot deep in some parts.

That is a lot of water!

In summer, do you go swimming?
Where is your favorite place to go?

FUN FACTS

The swimming pool, ilso called an Artificial Lagoon, made it into the Guinness Book of World Records. In 2019 this title went to another artificial lagoon in Egypt...

Some of the other sports that are popular in Chile are soccer and emboque.

The soccer team is commonly known as La Roja or the Red Team because of their bright red uniform.

Emboque is a typical children's game. The player must get a ball into a wooden cone. Another name for this game is called Ball in a Cup.

A few other sports that are played in Chile are:
- Volleyball
- Tennis and
- Water sports

Is there a special game that children play in your country?

FUN FACTS

Another game that is played often in Chile is *trompo*. Trompo is one of the oldest games played. It is the same as the spinning top.

The Chileans have a very unusual traditional dance called the Cueca. In the dance, the two dancers play the part of a rooster and hen. When they start dancing, they use a handkerchief which they twirl in the right hand.

You will often see this performed during the celebrations on September 18, in a festival called Fiestas Patrias.

There are quite a few different festivals celebrated throughout Chile, including on Easter Island. During the grape festival, a peasant couple crushes grapes to celebrate the wonder of Chilean wine. On Easter Island the Tapati Festival is colorful and magical, and there is also the Quasimodo festival where priests bring holy communion to the sick and are escorted by bandana-wearing horsemen.

What is your national dress like where you live?
When do you wear it?

Dress Up Time
Can you find the different pieces of clothing that make up the national dress of both your country and Chile? You might need an adult's help to find the right items.

FUN FACTS

The best place to see the national dress, the Pollera, is during the Cueca dance. The Pollera is worn by the woman and is made of vibrant colors and patterns. The Pollera is a skirt made from wool or cotton.

One of the festivals held celebrates Chilean wine, which comes from the beautiful grapes that grow in Chile.

Chile has the ideal climate and landscape to grow grapes, and produce wine. The most common wines in Chile are Cabernet Sauvignon, Merlot, and Carmenere.

Chile also exports a lot of its grapes. In 2022 Chile exported 66 920 662 boxes of grapes that weighed nearly 8.2kgs. That is a lot of grapes!

Do you know what resources are shared with other places from your Country?

FUN FACTS

Another resource that is in large quantities is Copper. Chile has the world's largest copper mine. You can find copper in electric wiring, as well as in radiators, heating and air-conditioners.

In Chile there are a few places that are looked after by UNESCO. UNESCO stands for the United Nations Educational, Scientific, and Cultural Organization.

Some of UNESCO's sites are:
- Rapa Nui National Park
- Churches of Chiloe
- The Historic Quarter of the Seaport City of Valparaiso
- Sewell Mining Archaeological Site for the Chinchorro Culture.

Looking at your country do you have any UNESCO sites?

FUN FACTS

UNESCOs mission is to help build peace, remove poverty, and communicate through education, science, culture, and information.

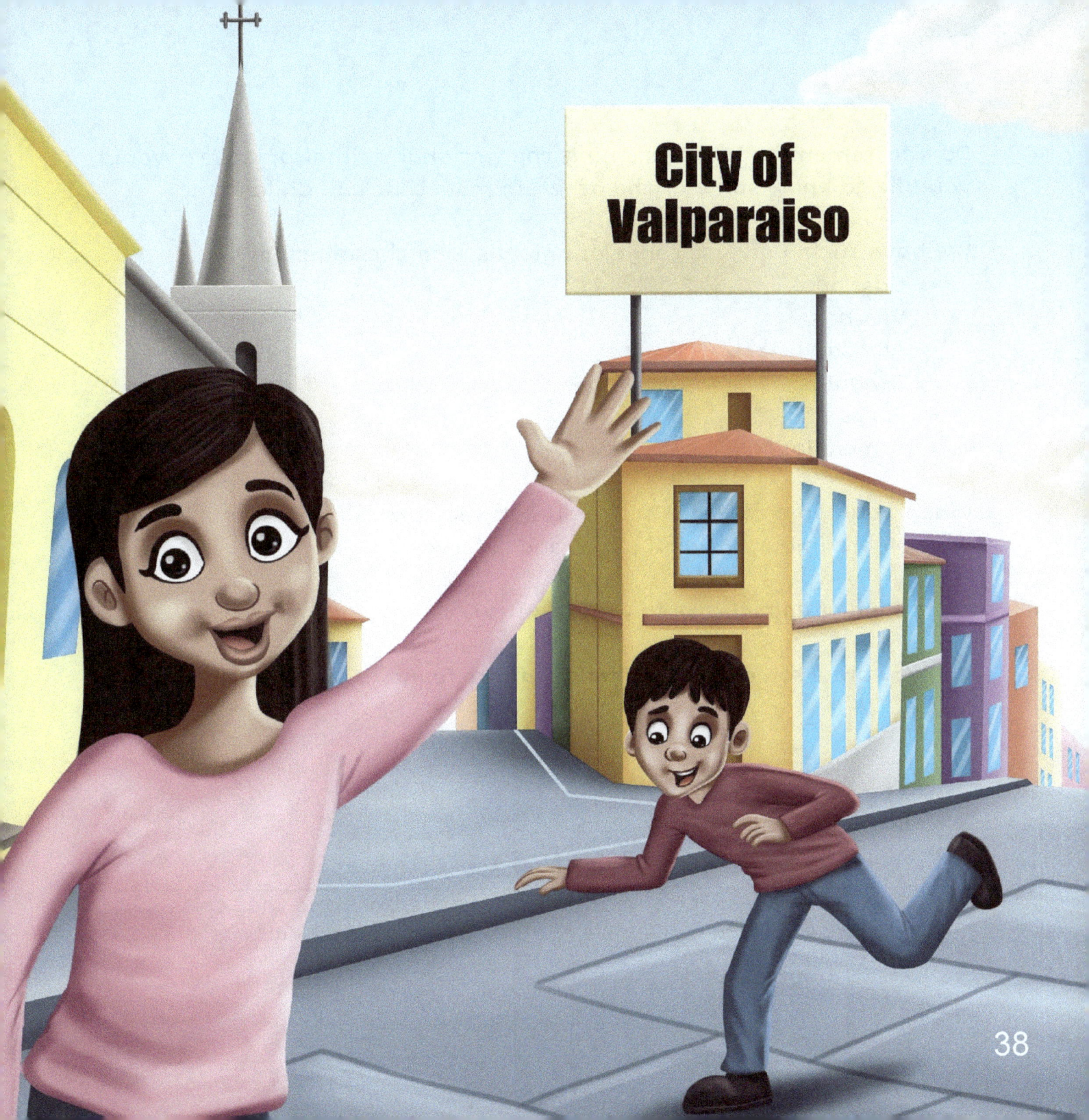

Do you remember us mentioning the national animal of Chile? Would you like to know some of the other animals that call Chile home?

We have such a diverse range of animals, and these include:
- Guanacos
- Vicunas
- Alpacas
- Penguins
- Foxes and
- Armadillos

When you come to visit Chile, you can see some of these animals and many more in our national parks and reserves.

What kind of animals live in your country?

Can you draw some of the animals that are found in Chile??

FUN FACTS

The Guanacos is a species of Llama and is the only one that spits. They are also related to Camels, Llamas, Alpacas, and Vicunas.

Chile has a range of mountains that are called the Andes.

Some interesting facts about the Andes that we would like to share with you are:

- In the South, the Andes are home to the world's highest volcano. The volcano is called Nevados Ojos del Salado.
- The highest volcano is also home to the highest lake. Ojos del Salado. It is a small lake that sits on the east side of the volcano.
- The longest river in Chile is called the Loa River, and it starts in the Andes.
- The Andes has the most famous landmark in Chile, the Torres del Paine National Park. There are some amazing things to see in this national park, including glaciers.

What other interesting facts can you find about The Andes?

With an adult's help and supervision, can you make a miniature Active volcano?

FUN FACTS

If you can measure from the center of the earth to Mount Chimborazo in the Andes, you would find the planet's tallest point. When families come to visit Easter Island, we encourage them to go on a treasure hunt.

There are so many fun things to do in Chile. You can go for a swim, paddle a kayak, climb or ski the Villarrica Volcano, or go white water rafting.

These are family-friendly activities, but there is so much more to explore! You can visit the museums or parks in Santiago, or talk a walk in the rainforest at the Huilo-hullo Biological Reserve.

Do you know that the ancient form of writing was drawing pictures?

How many different places can you find that have used drawing pictures to tell stories?

FUN FACTS
Easter Island is host to ancient petroglyphs. Petroglyphs are pictures that tell stories and date as far back as the history of Easter Island started. That's a long time.

Chile is well known for its work in literature. There have been many different ones that have created some amazing works of literature. Gabriela Mistral won a Nobel Laureate in 1945 for her works of Poetry. In 1971 Pablo Neruda won the Nobel Prize in Literature.
Literature is really important and essential to the Culture of Chile. It is classified as one of Chiles's national treasures.

> That is a big word! Can you help our readers with how to say literature and the meaning of the word?

> I sure can!
> To say literature, you break it down like this:
> li-tuh-ruh-chur
> It does not look like how it is spelled.
> Literature is anything that has been written. Things like stories and poems.

Now that you know what literature is, do you have any favorite books or poems?
Time to put on your thinking cap!
Can you write a poem about some of the things you have learned about Chile?

FUN FACTS

> Chile is sometimes called the Land of the Poets because of the success of Gabriela and Pablo.
>
> In Spanish Land of Poets is "el pais de poetas"

Another amazing part of Chile can be found in the skies above. Chile is the best place to go stargazing.

Many Astronomers or some who study the stars, love to come to Chile, and in particular the Atacama Desert to look at all the different stars. This is because the sky is really clear, and you can see without any pollution in the air.

Cities have too much pollution, or rubbish in the air, so it makes the air cloudy. But because the Atacama Desert does not have any cities, the air is really clean.

Astronomers love having clean air because they can see the stars clearly.

Where you live, can you see the stars?
Can you name any constellations, or star patterns?

Can you ask an adult if there is an observatory where you live?
If there is, see if you can go and have a look with the big telescope.
The telescope makes it easier to see the stars.

FUN FACTS
Chile is home to nearly 40 universities and observatories, making it the world's center to study Astronomy.

Mattias and I nearly forget to mention the money that is in Chile! We use the Peso.

The symbol for the peso is the $ and is known around the world as CLP.

There are 5 bank notes, and the amounts are:
- $1 000
- $2 000
- $5 000
- $10 000 and
- $20 000

Coins are hardly used in Chile, and only come in:
- 10
- 50
- 100 or
- 500 pesos

Do you know the history of your country's money?

FUN FACTS

Chile has changed its currency twice, originally from the Peso to the Escudo, and then back to the Peso.

In Chile, we tend to have small families. Sometimes we have one sibling, and sometimes we are on our own.

Most of the time, it is the dad that goes to work, and the mum stays at home looking after the children.

Women are encouraged to work, and to be proud of their accomplishments, but many women prefer to have traditional roles. Traditional roles mean that they prefer to stay at home, and help raise the children.

What type of family structure does your family have?
You will need to research the different types to find
Out what structure your family is.

FUN FACTS
Families in Chile have the family structure of a Nuclear Family. There are 7 different types of family structures.

Like many other countries, Chile has the following educational tiers:
- Primary Education
- Secondary Education
- Vocational Education and
- Tertiary Education

Attending primary and secondary school is required by law. Most of the education costs are paid by the government.

Do you know what the oldest school is where you live?

FUN FACTS

The oldest Chilean university is the *Universidad de Chile* established in 1622. It underwent 2 name changes during the time that it has been opened.

The temperature in Chile can vary between 28c in January and 11c in July.

Summer lasts from December to February, Autumn is from March to May, Winter is from June to August, and Spring is from September to November.

The summers here in Chile are mild, and we do not get too hot, and our winters are very wet. We have a lot of rain in winter.

Do you live in the Northern or Southern Hemisphere?

FUN FACTS

Seasons in the Northern Hemisphere are reversed to the seasons in the Southern Hemisphere.

Chile is a healthy country. Most of those that get sick in Chile are sick because of:
- high blood pressure
- Diabetes and
- Heart diseases.

Chile is super healthy because they have a great healthcare system, and because of the diet that is eaten.

How many hospitals are in the country that you live in?

FUN FACTS

In Latin America, there are over 18 000 hospitals within the 15 countries that call Latin America home.

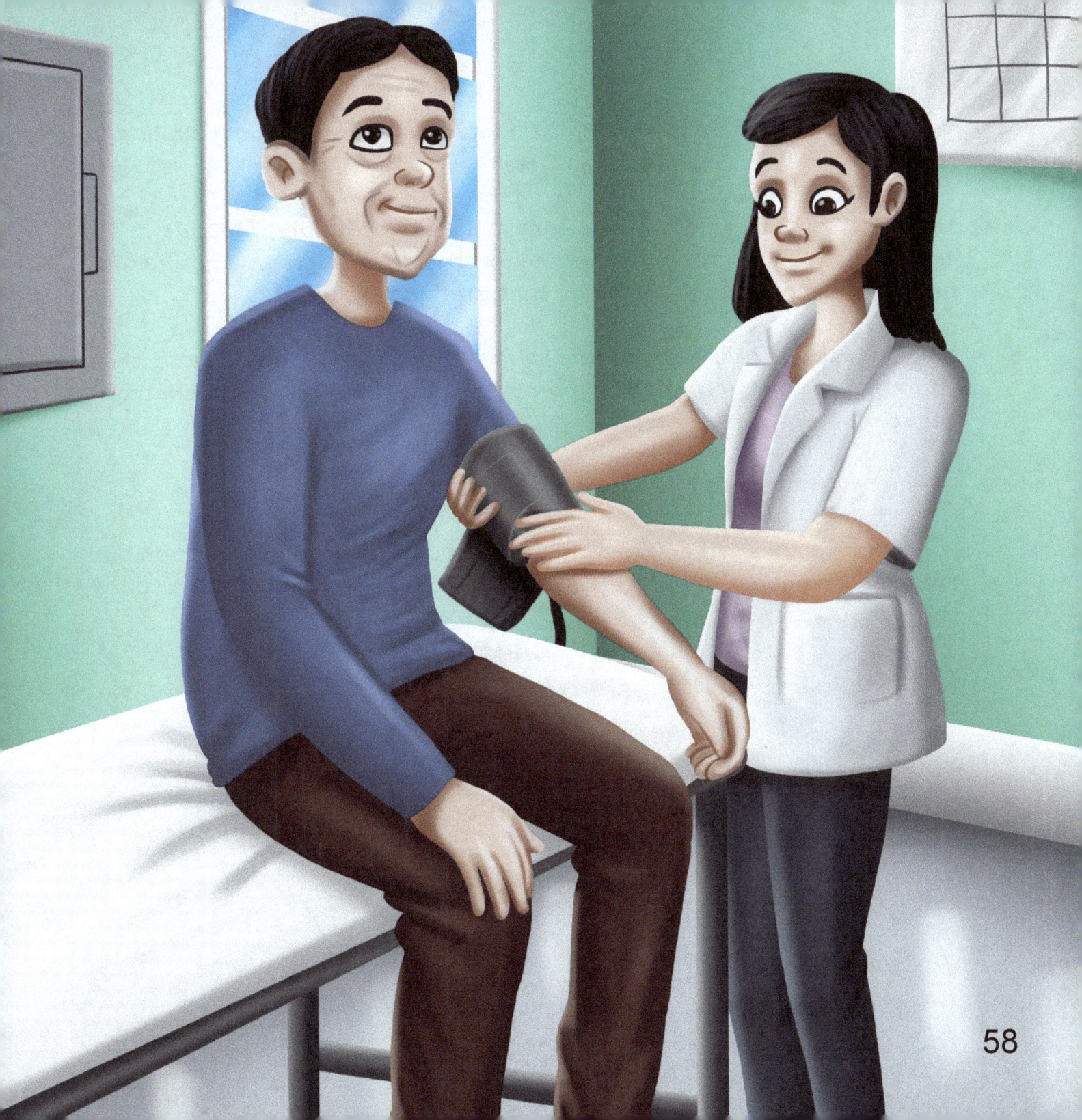

You have made it to the end! Did you have fun learning about Chile and learning some new and exciting facts?

There is so much to do and so many places to explore, Mattias and I encourage you to have a look at the internet with a grown-up's help to find all the places and fun things that are hidden away.

Chile is just one of the many fine jewels in the World, and we hope that you enjoyed your journey finding out some of the treasures that our beautiful home offers.

We just wish we had more time to tell you more!

Look out for the other Kids on Earth books, and meet some of our amazing neighbors and other jewels and treasures that can be found throughout the world.

Visit us at www.senseipublishing.com and sign up for our newsletter to learn more about our exciting books and to experience our **FREE Guided Meditations for Kids & Adults**.

As always...

It's a great day to be alive!

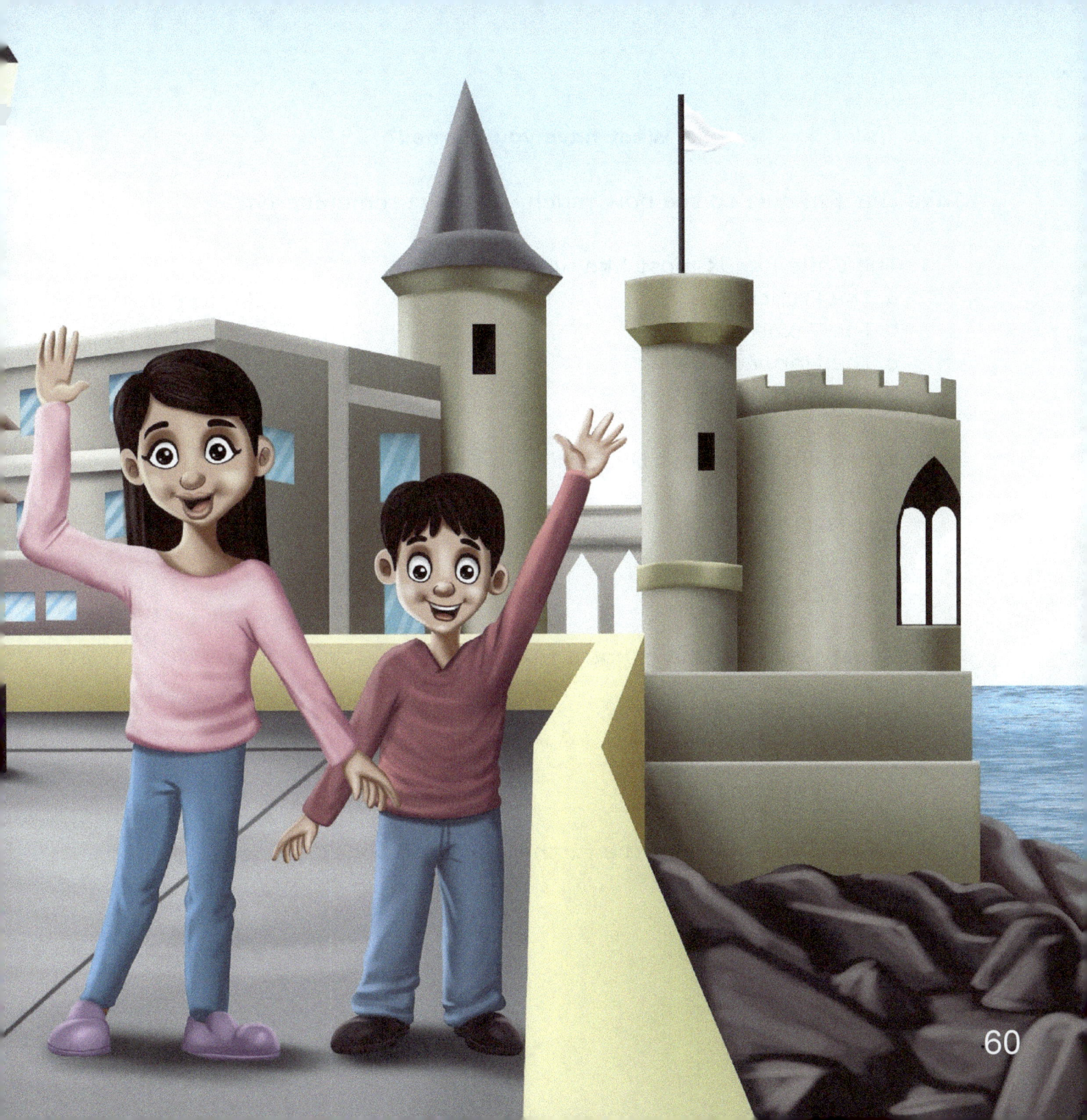

What have you learned?

Take this fun quiz to see how much you have remembered.

1. The Chile flag is most like which flag?
   a. The French Flag
   b. The Texas Flag
   c. The Norwegian Flag
   d. The Australian Flag

2. When did the oldest University in Chile open?
   a. 1622
   b. 1632
   c. 1602
   d. 1612

3. Which one of these is *not* a fruit?
   a. Avocado
   b. Tomato
   c. Carrot
   d. Pumpkin

4. What is the name of the farthest part of Chile?
   a. Andes
   b. Easter Island
   c. Greater Santiago
   d. Atacama

5. What are 2 of the games played in Chile?
    a. Chess and Knuckles
    b. Emboque and Trompo
    c. Cards and Table Tennis
    d. Bingo and Hangman

6. What is the smallest cat's breed name?
    a. Puma
    b. Serval
    c. Kodkod
    d. Bobcat

7. What can you share with your friends that you have learned from this book?

Quiz Answers: 1B, 2A, 3C, 4B, 5B, 6C

Share Our FREE eBooks Now!

kidsonearth.life

kidsonearth.world

Click Below for Another Book In Each Series

senseipublishing.com/KoE_SERIES

senseipublishing.com/KoE_Wildlife_SERIES

KoE En Español

senseipublishing.com/KoE_SERIES_SPANISH

www.senseipublishing.com

www.senseipublishing.com

@senseipublishing
#senseipublishing

Check out our **recommendations** for other books for adults & kids plus other great resources by visiting
www.senseipublishing.com/resources/

Join Our Publishing Journey!

If you would like to receive FREE BOOKS and special offers, please visit www.senseipublishing.com and join our newsletter by entering your email address in the pop-up box

Get Our FREE Books Today!

Click & Share the Links Below

FREE Kids Books

kidsonearth.world

kidsonearth.life

FREE BONUS!!!

Experience Over 25 FREE Engaging Guided Meditations!

Prized Skills & Practices for Adults & Kids. Help Restore Deep Sleep, Lower Stress, Improve Posture, Navigate Uncertainty & More.

Download the Free Insight Timer App and click the link below:

http://insig.ht/sensei_paul

About Sensei Publishing

Sensei Publishing commits itself to hhelppeople of all ages transform into better versions of themselves by providing high-quality and research-based self-development books with an emphasis on mental health and guided meditations. Sensei Publishing offers well-written e-books, audiobooks, paperbacks ,and online courses that simplify complicated but practical topics in line with its mission to inspire people towards positive transformation.

It's a great day to be alive!

About the Author

I create simple & transformative eBooks & Guided Meditations for Adults & Children proven to help navigate uncertainty, solve niche problems & bring families closer together.

I'm a former finance project manager, private pilot, jiu-jitsu instructor, musician & former University of Toronto Fitness Trainer. I prefer a science-based approach to focus on these & other areas in my life to stay humble & hungry to evolve. I hope you enjoy my work and I'd love to hear your feedback.

- It's a great day to be alive!
Sensei Paul David

Scan & Follow/Like/Subscribe: Facebook, Instagram: @kidsonearth

Scan using your phone/iPad camera for Social Media

Visit us at www.senseipublishing.com and sign up for our newsletter to learn more about our exciting books and to experience our FREE Guided Meditations for Kids & Adults.

www.ingramcontent.com/pod-product-compliance
Lightning Source LLC
Chambersburg PA
CBHW080022110526
44587CB00021BA/3736